We Are All Different

And We Are All Right

Written by

Elisabeth Norman Gardner

Illustrated by Rachel R. Lindsey

AuthorHouse™
1663 Liberty Drive
Bloomington, IN 47403
www.authorhouse.com
Phone: 1 (800) 839-8640

Published by AuthorHouse 04/23/2015

ISBN: 978-1-5049-0817-7 (sc)
ISBN: 978-1-5049-0819-1 (hc)
ISBN: 978-1-5049-0818-4 (e)

Library of Congress Control Number: 2015906193

Print information available on the last page.

Any people depicted in stock imagery provided by Thinkstock are models,
and such images are being used for illustrative purposes only.
Certain stock imagery © Thinkstock.

This book is printed on acid-free paper.

authorHOUSE®

Dedication

This book is dedicated, with love, to my grandchildren, Sam, Layton, Lori,
Lily and Camille, with the utmost hopes that you never suffer an encounter
with a bully and the utmost prayer that you NEVER become one!

A special, heartfelt dedication to Allison Graves Cheatwood, President of Have a
Heart Animal Rescue in Birmingham, AL., for saving Frankie from the shelter, trusting
me to foster him, working alongside me to get him healthy and, especially, for not
saying "I told you so" when I was a foster fail and asked to adopt him! Your love for
animals, coupled with your determination to help them, restores my faith daily.

With Special Thanks

To my husband, Paul, for his constant love and reassurance, offering assistance
when I needed it, space when I didn't and praise once the book was complete.

To my daughter, Molly for paying me the best compliment of all when she
read the first draft and stated "It's good Mom, I would buy it!"

To Joey Kennedy, journalist, friend and mentor, for his endless encouragement,
edits and downright indignant insistence that this story needed to be told.

To Rachel Lindsey, my amazing illustrator. She captured each of my animal's
personalities so beautifully, making us feel their heartache and rejoice in their victory!

And to Frankie, the wonderfully loving and ever-present inspiration for this book,
for his perseverance, his patience and his purrs in spite of the small helpings of
diet food. He now weighs a much healthier 20 pounds and is still dieting.

Foreword
By Joey Kennedy, Pug-daddy and Pulitzer Prize Winner

When I was young, and that was a long time ago, there was this one kid who enjoyed making life hard for a few of us who didn't fit in. He made sure our lives were miserable.

He was a bully.

Nothing I've read since then has had the impact that Elisabeth Norman Gardner's Frankie stories have had. These dogs and cats come from a hard life. These are about her animals and about our lives. They are us.

I've met Elisabeth's animals. I have visited with them in person. Once terribly overweight, Frankie the cat is awesome. But Frankie isn't alone: He's joined by Gabby and Joe and Pearl and others in the Gardner home. They are good souls from a bad situation. Like Frankie, they are rescued.

They are rescued!

According to statistics available, it is estimated that 160,000 children miss school every day due to fear of attack or intimidation by other students. American schools harbor approximately 2.1 million bullies and 2.7 million of their victims. One in 7 students in grades K-12 is either a bully or a victim of bullying. Fifty-six percent of students have personally witnessed some type of bullying at school. Fifteen percent of all school absenteeism is directly related to fears of being bullied at school. Seventy-six percent of students report incidents of bullying as a problem at their school.

This has to stop.

I believe Elisabeth's great mantra: We are ALL different, and we are ALL right.

Yes.

Life was always tough for me
Without a friend by my side,
I couldn't face all the jokes,
There was no place I could hide!

You see, I'm a very big boy,
Seems every week I would gain,
Then they laughed even more
And I ate to ease the pain.

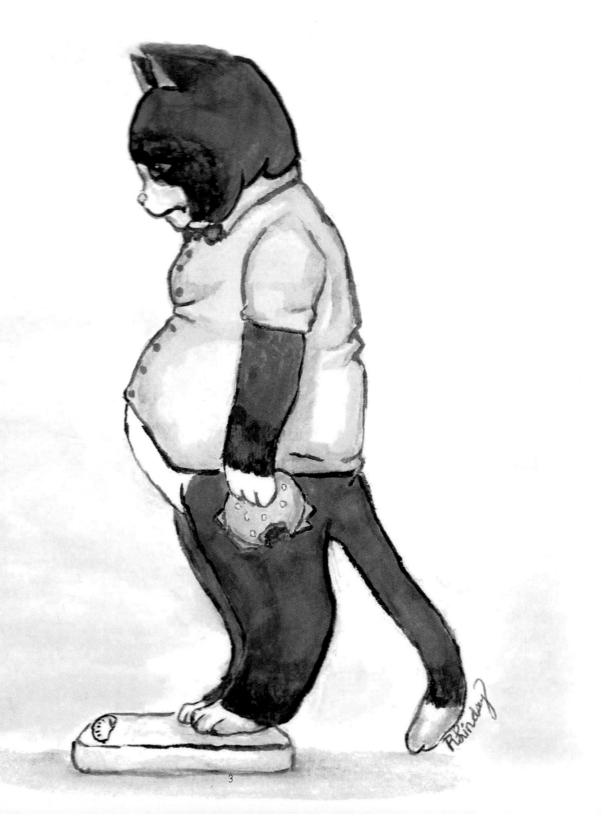

I tried hard to exercise
I even tried eating a small meal!
I couldn't change who I was,
I didn't know how to feel!

Then, I saw her crouched in a corner,
A very freckled little girl,
She was hiding her face
As she whispered "My name is Pearl".

The other kids taunted
"Hey, can I connect all your dots?"
She tried hiding them and bleaching them,
She even tried scrubbing off her spots!

We had something in common
In our club made of two.
We looked out for each other
And a strong friendship grew.

We built one another up
"You look great" we would say!
One day, a tiny girl approached us,
"Do you mind if I play?"

I had seen her before
She was always quite mean,
She was known for her fierceness.
There were fights I had seen!

I said "We don't want any trouble,
We are happy right here"
Gabby replied, "Please let me join you,
I'm so tired of living in fear!"

That's when we REALLY saw her,
a sweet girl, barely five,
She was so full of love
But she had to fight to survive!

The kids teased her and laughed
at her tiny body and big ears.
She lashed out and she fought them,
They wouldn't bring her to tears!

It seemed something was happening
We welcomed Gabby into our fold,
Promising to always protect her,
Who knew WE could be so bold?

Now, we needed a slogan,
Our club would be known near and far.
We could make people feel worthy,
Everyone would KNOW who we are!

25

We would no longer be silent,

We wouldn't stay hidden out of sight,

We would yell out our slogan

"We are ALL different and we are ALL right!"

He was watching from the distance,

Twisting his beautiful blonde curls,

He was laughed at and teased

Because he liked to play with the girls.

He said "My name is Joe,
But they call me Josephine!
I'm trying to like who I am,
Why do they have to be so mean?"

"May I stay here with you?
I think you understand".
"Joe, you're welcome in our club!"
And tiny Gabby held his hand.

The people kept coming,
Our new club was a hit!
Delilah found the courage to approach
"I'm not sure where I fit".

She said "My Mommy has black fur
And my Daddy's fur is white.
I always felt out of place
But, I'm just different, and it's ALL right!"

More classmates joined in a hug,

Even the Mean Willadeen!

She said "I will never bully again!"

It was the sweetest thing I had ever seen!

So, take a long look in a mirror
You have to love who you see!
You're not like anyone else
Say real loud "I LOVE ME!"

It turned into a big party,

We all learned what it meant

To love the person that you are,

Because we are ALL different!

Printed in the United States
By Bookmasters